THE HOW AND WHY WONDER BOOK OF
HORSES

Written by
MARGARET CABELL SELF

Illustrated by
WALTER FERGUSON

Editorial Production:
DONALD D. WOLF

Edited under the supervision of
Dr. Paul E. Blackwood, Washington, D. C.

Text and illustrations approved by
Oakes A. White, Brooklyn Children's Museum, Brooklyn, New York

PRICE STERN SLOAN
Los Angeles

Introduction

In *The How and Why Wonder Book of Horses,* we are reminded that someone once said, "There is something about the outside of a horse that is good for the inside of the man." This belief is certain to be strengthened by reading this book. For the horse as man's constant friend and helper is made vividly clear. Young people who, by good fortune, already know horses through personal experiences can find new knowledge and insights of several kinds. And those who have not had direct experience with horses will surely gain a new interest.

This book is filled with answers to many questions about horses and their usefulness. For example, it tells how the horse has developed from primitive beginnings, when it was no larger than a fox, to the present day. And it describes how, by careful selection and breeding, horses for different purposes have been developed.

We do not always think about the importance of this animal to the history of mankind. Yet, because of its speed, strength and intelligence the horse has uniquely changed the course of history. Without it there would have been no Pony Express! And without it the movement to the great prairies of the West would have been greatly delayed. Yes, the horse and the history of mankind are closely related.

The How and Why Wonder Book of Horses has value for use in history and social classes as well as in science. And equally important, it can be read and enjoyed just for the fun of it.

Paul E. Blackwood

Dr. Blackwood is a professional employee in the U. S. Office of Education. This book was edited by him in his private capacity and no official support or endorsement by the Office of Education is intended or should be inferred.

Contents

The Beginning of Horses

Many millions of years ago a tiny creature no larger than a fox ran across the plains of North America. It had four soft toes on its feet and is known as *eohippus*. The skeletal remains of eohippus have many things in common with the skeletal structure of the modern horse, especially in the type and distribution of

What animal was the earliest ancestor of the modern horse?

their teeth. This is how we know that eohippus is the direct ancestor of today's horse even though the two don't look much alike.

To answer this question we must think a little about what the problems of eohippus were and how the creature reacted to them. The animal was small, and no doubt its flesh

Why did eohippus change?

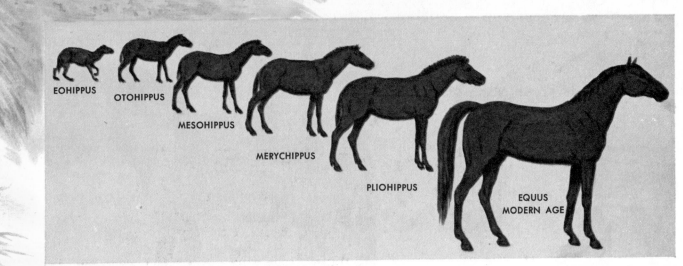

EOHIPPUS
OTOHIPPUS
MESOHIPPUS
MERYCHIPPUS
PLIOHIPPUS
EQUUS
MODERN AGE

The development of the horse from the fox-sized eohippus to the pony-like *Equus* was a process that took millions of years.

Dinictis was a primitive saber-toothed tiger. It is shown chasing a group of Dawn Horses. The Dawn Horse, or eohippus, was the earliest known ancestor of the modern horse.

was tasty. The larger meat-eating animals must have considered it a very delicious morsel. But little eohippus had no weapons of defense against its many enemies. It did not have the tearing fangs and claws of the cat family which included the tigers, lions and leopards. It had no hard shell like the turtle, nor thorny spines like the porcupine and hedgehog. Its feet were soft, as it did not have the hard hoofs of today's horses. The only thing it could do in the face of danger was to run away. So run it did, century after century.

Now, it is far easier to run on tiptoe than it is to run "flat-footed." Since eohippus ran on tiptoe, it was a better runner than flat-footed animals and was successful, for the most part, in escaping enemies. Its outside toes were hardly used at all, and as the centuries passed, these toes became smaller and smaller, while the middle toes continued to develop. Mutations, or changes, take place constantly in all species, and any change that improved the development of the center toes would give eohippus an advantage.

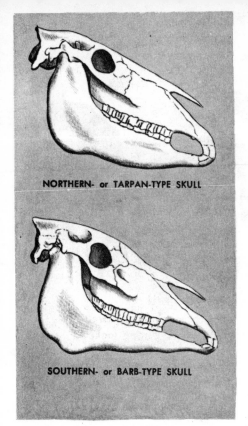

NORTHERN- or TARPAN-TYPE SKULL

SOUTHERN- or BARB-TYPE SKULL

The Tarpan, or *Equus Przhevalski,* the Wild Horse of Asia, today looks exactly as it did a million years ago. It inhabits the steppes of Tartary and Mongolia from the Dnieper to the Altai Mountains and roams the vast area of central Asia.

Millions of years later, eohippus had changed so completely that it got a new name — *pliohippus.* This is the first of the prehistoric horses that began to bear any resemblance to the horses of today. It was still very small, but the center toe of each foot was now very long and was beginning to develop a thick, horny nail, while the side toes had all but disappeared.

Since running away was still its only means of defense, pliohippus, like its ancestor, was always on the alert. If the animal suspected danger, it ran.

It is this characteristic which makes the

Why is the horse useful to man?

horse useful to man. One cannot use a steer or a cow for sport or for swift transportation. A steer has horns and its reaction in the face of danger is not to run but to stand still and fight. It is therefore not as timid or sensitive as the horse and not so easily trained, nor has it ever developed the horse's speed and natural agility.

It is true that oxen are used as farm animals, and so are camels and other animals, but they could never replace the horse which can be used for heavy labor, too. But more important, the horse has been man's friend and servant in war and his companion and playmate in sport for many centuries.

Did all horses look alike in early times?

Animals develop according to their environment and inherited make-up. If there is plenty to eat they increase in size up to a point. If they do a great deal of

6

Equus robustus, or Great Horse of Europe, looked much like our draft horses of today. Big, but not clumsy, it was trained to move fast.

running their leg muscles become very strong. Their color varies, depending on where they live, for nature usually provides a natural disguise, especially for those animals which have few other defensive weapons.

Forty million years ago there were parts of the earth that were very cold, barren wastes with little food for animals. Other parts were swampy with rich vegetation. Still others had grassy plains. Sometimes the climate of a specific region changed due to the tremendous shifting of glaciers and all forms of natural food disappeared. In this case the primitive horse migrated or even died out completely.

Which types of horses sprang from *Equus*? The first horse that really resembled those of today was named *Equus*. It lived first in North America, but when shifting glaciers and ice changed the

weather, *Equus* migrated to South America. It also went into Asia and thence to Europe and to Africa. *Equus* looked much like the ponies of today and had a flying mane and tail and a hard hoof. From *Equus* four main types of horses, which formed the basis of modern breeds, developed. In Asia, where the climate was very cold, where there was little forage, and great barren wastes as well as rocky mountains, two wild horses developed. One of these is called the *tarpan* and it is the only horse today that looks exactly as it did a million years ago. It is mouse-colored with a stripe down its back. The tarpan has a strong, chunky body, short legs, a coarse heavy head and a shaggy coat. It is virtually untamable in the wild state, but has been crossed with other strains to provide mounts and draft horses.

Another type is the dun-colored *Przhevalski's horse* — named after the Russian discoverer — or the "horse of

7

The Roman light cavalry in action. The riders had no saddle and stirrups, and though they had reins, the horses obeyed light signals of weight and legs, which left the hands free for combat.

This is an Egyptian chariot of the fourteenth century B.C. Much information has been gained from a study of the bas-reliefs of chariots found on the walls of ancient Egyptian tombs.

Pegasus was the winged horse of Greek myth.

Alexander the Great rode his horse, Bucephalus.

This is a fifteenth century mounted battle horse.

the steppes." It is more easily tamed than the tarpan. In its natural habitat it is very strong and swift, though small, being only about forty-eight inches at the shoulder. These little ponies, even when stabled, groomed and fed, usually degenerate and are not as strong nor as swift as their wild brothers.

In Europe where the climate was mild and food was plentiful, there developed a horse called the *Equus robustus* or "Great Horse." It looked much like our draft horses of today. It was used by the knights, for with their heavy armor a very big, strong horse was necessary. Although it was big, it was not clumsy, and *Equus robustus* was trained to move very quickly and cleverly.

In Africa and in certain parts of central Europe a slender, swift-moving animal known as *Equus agilis* roamed the plains. It is from this horse that we get the *Arabian, Barb* and *Andalusian* strains as well as the *Greek* horses. *Equus agilis* is the ancestor of all the horses of today known as the "light" breeds. We shall learn how man, through selective breeding, has developed the modern horse so that it can be used for specific purposes and, in so doing, has changed its appearance and temperament.

Ponies developed in the islands of Europe. They survived on

Where did ponies come from?

sparse food supplies because they were small and needed little food. The *Shetlands,* the basic strain, came from the "Great Horse" and they are built exactly like their big cousin. Some

9

of the other breeds, such as the *Welsh* and *Dartmoor* ponies lived in more open country and had Arabian blood introduced purposely so that they are much slimmer. Many people think that all ponies are stubborn and not to be trusted. This is not true. Ponies are kind by nature but easily spoiled. Properly trained and disciplined they make fine pets and good mounts for the young child. But ponies are strong and intelligent. They soon learn that if the child who tries to ride or drive them is incompetent they can do what they want. No child should try to manage either a pony or a horse until he has been taught "horse language." He has to learn how to sit correctly and "talk" to his horse through the use of his hands, weight and legs.

The use by man of the horse has af-

What is the horse's most valuable characteristic?

fected the development of mankind and nations more than any other factor. The ancient Sanskrit word for swiftness is *asva* and this is what the Mesopotamians called the horse. The Greek *equus* was taken from the word *acer,* also meaning "quickness." So we know that from the beginning man realized the horse's most valuable characteristic — speed.

The Horse in Battle

Before man learned to ride he discov-

How did the horse figure in mythology?

ered that the horse could be used to draw a rough chariot which, in turn, was useful both in warfare and in sport. Once this discovery was made the horse became very important indeed. Since, in ancient times, things of importance were immediately incorporated into the pagan religions, we find the horse prominent in mythology. The sun was all important so the sun-god is to be found in all early religions and mythologies. Indra, the colorful sun-god of India, drove a flaming chariot across the sky drawn by mighty horses. The Greek god Apollo did likewise. Even Poseidon, the

god of the sea, is depicted as being carried everywhere by his white-maned steeds, the crashing waves. Indeed, we speak of that part of the horse's neck which curves, as the *crest*, just as we speak of the "crest" of a wave. Individual horses were also mentioned in mythology. Pegasus, the winged horse of the Greeks, is the best known.

The early chariots of the Europeans and Asians were **What were the early chariot teams like?** badly designed and balanced. They were drawn by teams of two or more horses and contained a driver, a soldier who fought, and sometimes one or more others who protected the first two. The horses were taught to charge without the restraint of reins. Though one sometimes sees reins in early drawings, these are usually shown

fastened to the side of the chariot, the driver evidently controlling his mounts with his voice and urging them on with a whip. The Assyrians developed a well-designed chariot and all the nations of that time depended on their chariots to win battles.

The earliest written records of systematic training of the horse that we have are the Hittite tablets, engraved on stone more than three thousand years ago. They give a definite program for the selection, testing, conditioning and care of the horse to be used in battle. But long before this era, artists were drawing pictures and making sculptures of horses both hitched to chariots and ridden.

The light cavalry of the early nations **What did the light cavalry consist of?** consisted of men riding horses without saddles or stirrups and generally without reins. Horses are easily trained to obey light signals of weight and knee and the Assyrians, Greeks and other peoples took advantage of this, for it left their hands free for fighting. In the first battles the commanders of the armies used the chariots arrayed abreast in a solid wall to charge the enemy and mow them down. Sometimes sharp knives were fastened to the hub caps of the wheels. Nothing could withstand the assault of the powerful, galloping, uncontrolled animals. When the dust had died down, the light cavalry rode in to finish off the survivors, assisted by the charioteers who had turned and were going over the battlefield again.

It was Alexander the Great who first used horses in a different way. He had a great sympathy and love for horses and was a famed horseman. At thirteen he was given Bucephalus, a supposedly untamable black stallion, which he trained without using harsh methods. In a famous battle, Alexander found himself facing a vast army ten times greater than his own. Its chieftain had assembled four miles of elephants as well as thousands of war chariots and light cavalry. But Alexander so maneuvered his few mounted men that they attacked from both sides and from behind at the same time. Since neither the elephants nor the chariots could be turned quickly, they only hindered the light cavalry of the enemy army and Alexander won the battle.

In medieval times the knights wore

What kind of horse did the knights ride?

heavy armor to protect themselves from stones and arrows. Now the individual became important as a fighter. Only two skills were necessary for the knight: he had to know how to use a sword and how to ride a horse. In several languages the very word for gentleman is the same as that for horseman. Thus we have the *chevalier* of France and the *caballero* of Spain. The horses that the knights rode were very big and heavy, similar to the draft horses of today, but they were highly trained and far from clumsy.

Only in Arabia was the small, lightly-built horse valued. This was because the Arabians never wore armor. There the horse was considered so important that it became a member of the household, often lying down beside its master in the tent. Furthermore, it was trained not only to carry its rider, but also to act as watchdog and warn him of the approach of enemies. Because the Arab had such a close association with his mount, the Arabian horses, though nervous and high-spirited, are the most willing, trusting and intelligent of any breed of horse.

With the invention of gunpowder, the

Why did the horse cavalry disappear?

armor and the knights disappeared and modern cavalry was adopted by all nations. But later, tanks and other heavy armored vehicles took over. They could go over rough terrain, withstand shells and carry a number of men and their

PALFREY

COURSER

weapons, so that today we find the horse cavalry absent from the battlefield, a fact for which every horse lover is glad.

In medieval times there were no professional armies such as developed later. Rather, every man, when called upon, was expected to follow his king or lord into battle or on a Crusade. All except the serfs went mounted. The horseman, from his elevated position, had a great advantage over the foot-soldier. Therefore, every man who could afford to keep a horse had not one, but several. There was the *charger,* an enormously heavy animal used in tournaments, and the *courser,* a slightly lighter animal and even more highly trained, which was used in jousting and in hand-to-hand combat. In addition there were *palfreys,* horses with unusually smooth gaits. The knight rode one of these when he was not fighting. His squire also rode one as did his lady. Then there was his *battle horse,* another large animal which was used as a pack horse to carry extra equipment. It was led and not mounted.

Since the man's very life depended on the agility and training of his horse,

What kinds of horses were used in the Middle Ages?

the art of horsemanship and of training horses was very highly developed. Many centuries before, the Egyptians, Greeks and others had studied the natural movements of the horse. They then learned to train their animals to execute the same movements at the behest of the rider. On the Parthenon, the famous temple in Greece, we see the sculptures of a Greek artist which show the horse performing many complicated steps — while mounted and with the rider standing beside it. Early Egyptian vases also depict the training of the horse.

The knight trained horses too. For example, in battle he might find himself surrounded by foot-soldiers. He could cause his horse to sink back on its hind legs and remain perfectly immobile while he fought with his sword. This was called the *levade.* From this position the horse could rise high in the air and hop forward two or three steps. This was the *courbette,* from the French word meaning "crow." Having cleared a slight space in front of itself with this maneuver, the horse could then be made to come back to earth on all four feet, spring high in the

What were the horses of the knights trained to do in battle?

CHARGER

BATTLE HORSE

air, and kick straight back into the faces of the enemy. This was called the *capriole*. On landing, the horse would do a swift *pirouette* on one hind foot and charge out and away through the path it had cleared behind itself. How the knights maintained their seats, encumbered as they were by heavy armor, is a miracle, but their saddles were so built that they could only fall off sideways.

If you find it hard to believe that horses can be so trained, you have only to go to Vienna and see the famous *Lippizan* horses, which seem veritably to sprout wings when they execute these same movements. The knight used the courser for this work.

When there was not much happening

What was a tournament?

by way of excitement, the kings and lords would arrange tournaments to keep their knights in training and give them a chance to show off be-

fore the ladies as well. A suitable spot was chosen, the banners of the various contestants flew in the breeze, trumpeters filled the air with fanfares, and tents and stands were erected to accommodate the spectators. Now the knight rode his great charger, an animal chosen for its weight, strength and courage. It was not as swift or as agile as the courser, but it was well trained for the job.

The tournament was, in reality, a miniature battle. Supposedly it was just for fun, but it could be very rough and many men lost their lives. It started with two lines of knights drawn up at the opposite ends of the field. At a trumpet call, both lines moved forward at a gallop. The knights carried long, pointed spears. The horses were trained to go as close as possible to the opposing horse without actually touching it. Each knight tried to catch his opponent in the neck with the point of his spear and,

A joust was usually a mock combat fought on horseback between two or more knights wielding long lances.

if he succeeded, the impact of several tons of charging horse and man inevitably ended in one or both men being unhorsed. Often the horse, too, was thrown over backward, landing on top of its rider. Many riders found themselves unable to extricate themselves and died from the severe crush and suffocation. Meanwhile, those fortunate enough to have retained their seats turned and charged back again. This went on until only one rider was left. He now dismounted, his horse was led away, and everyone still able to do so drew his sword and continued the fight on foot.

Horses of the American West

In 1537, Cortez landed on the east

When were horses introduced to the American continent?

coast of what is now Mexico, bringing with him sixteen or eighteen horses. The native Indians had never before seen a horse. When they saw mounted men for the first time they took them to be gods with six legs and two heads and wanted to worship them. Not long after, nearly a thousand more horses were sent from Spain.

When Cortez left, having conquered the country and claiming it for Spain, he gave away some of his horses. Many others strayed away and they were either taken in by the Indians or migrated north where they ran wild. Soon there were bands of wild horses all over the West. It is from these animals that the wild *mustangs* are descended. The Cortez horses were of Arabian and Andalusian strains, their ancestors having been introduced into Spain from Arabia at the time of the Moslem conquests. They looked much like the stock horses of today and were sturdy, small and very self-sufficient. Those brought by Cortez were mostly chestnuts, duns, browns and greys.

Later, spotted horses appeared, a result of mutations, or changes, in the species. These became known as *pintos*, meaning "painted." The *palomino*, whose flying silver mane and tail and metallic gold color give him a tremendous appeal, originated in the court of Queen Isabella of Spain — the queen who sold her jewels in order to finance Christopher Columbus in his explorations. She had a personal bodyguard of these horses and they came to be known as *Ysabellas*.

What are pintos?

In addition to the ordinary use of the horse to carry its master in his travels, pull the plow and draw the family surrey to church on Sundays, horses had one or two special uses in the United States. When the rich prairies of the West were discovered, many people wanted to go there. The climate was milder, the soil richer and the rocks fewer than in New England. Since Indians ruled the land it was much safer for people to travel in large groups. So pioneers who wished to settle in the West assembled in frontier towns together with their families, all their movable property, their covered wagons and, most important of all, their horses.

How did the pioneers use horses?

Without the horses the migrations would have been impossible. Oxen were strong, it is true, but they could go only about four miles in a day. For a family of any size this meant carrying too large a supply of food to make it practical, though it is true some oxen were used. When several groups were ready they would set out in long trains, with the babies and elderly women riding in the great wagons, and everyone else riding or walking — and generally with the family cow tied on behind. Since there was no way of getting replenishments, every article needed in the new settlement as well as all grain for planting

The American Indian was famed as a bareback rider and hunter. His mount (left) is an Appaloosa of mixed color. The Conestoga wagon (above) was named after the city in Pennsylvania where it was manufactured.

had to be carried. The heavy wagons were made water-tight so that they could be floated across the mighty rivers which lay between the pioneers and their goal.

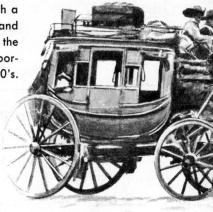

The stagecoach, with a team of four strong and fast horses, was the main form of transportation in the 1800's.

The best known of these wagons were

What kind of wagons did the pioneers use?

called *Conestogas* and the horses had the same name. The wagons were painted bright red and the wheels and underparts were blue. They had no seats and the driver sat on the left horse nearest the wheels. Four, six or more horses pulled a wagon. These horses were a general utility type suitable for work or as saddle animals. Ahead of the wagon train rode the scouts and behind it came the rear guard who brought along the cattle.

The Indians of those days were well

What kind of horses did the Indians ride?

mounted on horses that were descended from the Spanish horses. They rode as did the ancient Abyssinians and Egyptians — bareback and without bridles, since they needed both hands to handle their weapons. The Indians were superb horsemen and, like the Arabians, treated their horses as members of the family. The Indian ponies were small and tough, having run wild since the days of Cortez.

At night the pioneers formed their wagons in a great circle — with the people and animals inside — as a protection against possible Indian attack and to prevent the stealing of their livestock by the red men. But had it not been for the horse, the settling of the great prairies of the West would certainly have been greatly delayed.

The stagecoach got its name from the

What horses were used for stagecoaches?

fact that it went from one designated point to another — in stages — on a regular scheduled journey. As the coach with its four or more horses drew up to an inn, fresh relays of horses were brought out, while the tired ones were unhitched and put into the stable. The roads of Europe were often very heavy with mud and the coaches themselves were heavy vehicles loaded down with both passengers and baggage. The horses, therefore, had to be strong ones. But since speed was also essential, they could not be the slow-moving draft type of animal. Several different breeds were developed for this purpose.

In England a breed called the *Cleveland Bay* became popular, though it was never entirely successful. In France we had the *French Coach,* a breed derived from European mares and *Thoroughbred* stallions. They were beautiful-looking animals, but since the mares

18

FRENCH COACH

GERMAN COACH

were picked at random on their appearance alone—without regard to ancestry — the colts were often great disappointments. There was also a *German Coach* horse. It was never very popular, however, since its trot was not good and the animal was clumsy.

The most popular of the coach horses were the *Hackneys*. In fact, the best and fastest coaches were called *Hackney Coaches*. These horses had speed, style and strength. They were the result of a cross between the Thoroughbred stallion and the *Norfolk* mare. The latter was an English draft breed. Nearly all

private coaches and driving vehicles were pulled by Hackneys, which varied greatly in size.

In choosing horses to pull a coach, those next to the coach — called the *wheelers* — had to be very powerful animals. The early coaches had no brakes, and since the coachmen were inclined to take advantage of the regular stops to have a warming drink, they sometimes tried to make up for lost time by pushing the horses along at a gallop. On the hills, the weight plus the momentum of the loaded coach came to several tons and it took a strong pair of horses to sit back in the traces and

The Hackney, a coach horse, developed in England.

The Clydesdale (upper left), originating in Scotland, and the Belgian (lower left), developed in Belgium, are draft horses useful for drawing heavy loads. The horse-drawn streetcar was a familiar sight in our cities not long ago.

In Holland, horses still draw canal boats. The Shire (upper right) was developed in England and is the largest of the draft horses. The Percheron (lower right), a draft horse of France, is mild-mannered, agile and strong.

prevent the coach from getting entirely out of control. The lead horses, however, were not as heavy and they set the pace. Still, accidents were frequent and often fatal both to passengers and to horses.

The early mail coaches had what were

What is posting?

called *post-boys* who rode the near horses — those hitched on the left side. They managed both the horse they rode and its partner. They soon found out that they got less tired if, instead of sitting to the trot, they rose up and down in the saddle in cadence with the stride. This came to be known as *posting* to the trot and is so called today.

In the United States many coaching lines came into being, but most of them went quickly out again because there was too much competition. The roads were even worse than those in England and the horses soon died of overwork.

20

Early in the 1800's, both in Europe and

How were coaches the forerunners of the railroads?

the United States, it was discovered that fewer horses were needed to draw a coach. They could pull heavier loads and pull them faster if, instead of running on muddy roads, the coach was fitted with special wheels and drawn along parallel iron rails. The coaches were double-decker and the horses were usually hitched one in front of the other. This was the forerunner of the railroad. Its greatest disadvantage was that there were no regular schedules, and there was only a single track with an occasional turn-off. Two coaches traveling fast in opposite directions often met head-on with complete disaster to both. Sometimes, instead of actually colliding, both coachmen stopped their vehicles and everyone got out and had a fight. The losers were forced to back up to the nearest turn-off.

Horses were also used to pull the canal

How were horses used with the canal boats?

boats which had been built in many parts of the country. These were flat-bottomed boats which ran along an artificially constructed stream of water. Beside the stream was the tow-path, built from the dirt that was

The horses of the Pony Express were swift and tough.

dug out to make the canal. The boats were double-decker affairs where the ladies usually sat on the top deck chatting, knitting and enjoying the scenery. The gentlemen were more often to be found below deck at the bar or card tables. One or two horses pulled the boat by ropes attached to the prow and extra horses were carried aboard so that no animal worked too long at a time. Speed was not essential and the trip was as much a social outing as anything else.

When the West was partially settled, the

What was the Pony Express?

roads, particularly in the mountainous districts, became impassable in snowy or stormy weather. Yet communication, especially for business purposes, was essential. So in 1860, an organization known as the Pony Express came into being. Its purpose was to carry important documents from St. Joseph, Missouri to Sacramento, California in the shortest possible time. This was a distance of nearly

two thousand miles. The originator was William H. Russel, who bought five hundred of the toughest horses he could find and hired eighty of the strongest and smallest men available.

Stations were set up at ten- or fifteen-mile intervals where a blacksmith and two men were stationed. Their job was to care for the animals that were awaiting their turn to run and to have an animal saddled and outside the station when the horn of the approaching rider was heard. Since speed was the objective, only two and a half minutes were allowed for the transfer of the mail pouch — which was fastened to the saddle — and of the rider from his tired beast to his fresh replacement, and this was often accomplished in a minute or less. Each horse was kept at a full gallop for its full stint, regardless of road conditions. The riders were first asked to ride only four stages. Later this was increased to eight. One record mentions a man who rode a hundred miles a night for three successive nights each week,

then rested for two. He claims to have used the same horse, but if this is true, it was against the usual practice.

The horses were small, wiry mustangs.

What kind of horses were used by the Pony Express?

They were taught to run fast and to stay on the trail no matter what happened. In several instances the riders fell from the saddle from fatigue, but the horses continued on to the next station without hesitation. In one case the rider was shot by Indians and the horse brought the body and the mail pouch safely to the next station on time. The enterprise lasted only eighteen months when it was replaced by the railroad. It was a failure financially, although the postage charged was high — five dollars per half-ounce. But in that eighteen-month period, it built up a tremendous reputation and the term "Pony Express" became a synonym for speed, courage, endurance and fleetness of both horse and rider.

A-hunting We Will Go!

Early drawings that date about 800 B.C. show the Assyrians hunting stag and other animals with bows and arrows and with spears. In some pictures we see them mounted bareback. The horses wear bridles with what appear to be simple bar snaffles, but the reins are tied up and the rider is using both hands to

shoot. This indicates that, like the American Indian mounts, these horses were very obedient and highly trained. They reacted, even in the excitement of the chase, to signals given by the rider through his knees and the shifting of his weight. Other drawings of the Assyrians depict hunting parties riding in two-

Man probably hunted animals for food as long ago as 250,000 years or more. But hunting as a sport developed much later. England is, today, the center of fox hunting.

wheeled, well-designed chariots. One man drove while another, facing backwards, speared his prey.

In the Europe of early medieval times

What was the purpose of the fox hunt?

and later, each nobleman kept a private pack of hounds. His hunt servants wore a special livery, or uniform, so that they might be identified. The purpose of the hunt was to exterminate the foxes which were considered very destructive to poultry and game birds. Some noblemen kept stag hounds. With these they hunted stag both for sport and for venison. Hunting for wild boar was also a popular but dangerous sport.

In modern times, as far as fox hunting

What is a Hunt Club?

goes, the picture is much the same. However, there are few private hunts today. Instead, a group of people form a Hunt Club. They then get permission from neighboring landowners to ride over their properties. They assemble a pack of hounds and hire kennel men to take care of them. For Hunt Servants they choose a Master of Fox Hounds, called an "MFH" for short, two Whips and, if the MFH is not an experienced Huntsman, a professional Huntsman. In every country where fox hunting is a recognized sport, there is a National Association of Masters of Foxhounds. Before a Hunt Club

can be recognized it must apply to the National Association for permission. This is so there will not be too many Hunts in one locality.

Each Hunt has its own livery, just as

What is the clothing of the Hunt?

in the old days. This insures that the riders are well turned out and identifies them as members of the local Hunt Club. But a rider must prove himself before he is allowed to wear the Hunt colors. The first season he wears a plain black coat, a hard hat to prevent injuries from falls or overhead branches, a white stock tied in a special kind of knot and pinned with a plain gold safety pin, tan or brown breeches and high black boots. If he proves to be a worthy member, the Master, at the end of the season, will then invite him to wear the special livery of the club. For men this is often a bright red coat — called a "Pink" coat after a famous English tailor — a gay vest and special gold buttons with the Hunt initials on it. Ladies who are not members of the staff wear a black coat with a colored collar. The formal type of hat for members of the field is a high silk hat with a hard reinforcement. The Master, the Hunt Servants, children under eighteen and farmers wear a velvet cap, also reinforced. Everyone else wears a black bowler or derby.

The reason for this special livery is in-

What was the reason for the special clothing?

teresting. A bright-colored coat was chosen to avoid accidents, since a rider in red is more easily seen than one in brown or black. The white stock with the safety pin can serve as a sling or a bandage in case of accidents. In the old days, there used to be what was known as a "hat tax," and the money was used to help support the Hunt. Since the farmers were the ones over whose land the Hunt rode, they were not taxed. Children and members of the staff were also not taxed. The nontaxpayers wore special headgear to identify them, which made it easier for the Hunt Secretary who was responsible for collecting fees. Originally the fees were collected at the meeting place before the fox hunt started. The Huntsman or Sec-

retary went around and held out his cap for contributions. These fees are still called "capping fees." But nowadays all regular members pay an annual subscription.

The Huntsman, or Master if he is performing both duties, leads the hounds to a spot where there is good cover, a likely place in which a fox might hide. He encourages them, with voice and horn, to go into the brush and rout out Reynard. The Whips station themselves on each side of the *covert* (cover), as it is called.

What are the duties of the Hunt Staff?

When a fox is located all hounds are encouraged to collect together and go after it. When the fox runs out of the underbrush it is given time to get away, and then the hounds, followed by the MFH or Huntsman with the Whips riding on either flank to bring up any lazy hounds, take off at their heels.

Behind them rides the Field Master who is in charge of the "Field"; that is, the remaining followers of the Hunt. He sees that no one rides too close to the hounds so as to injure or frighten them, that no one interferes with the work of the other Hunt Servants, and that no one rides over freshly planted fields. All of the aforementioned people carry short wooden crops with hooks on one end and long leather thongs on the other. The hooks are useful for opening gates or catching a stray horse whose rider has come to grief — the thongs are used to discipline hounds. Many of the "Field" also carry these crops, called "hunt crops."

The hounds themselves have been carefully trained and disciplined to follow the scent of the fox and not to be detracted from it. They are the ones that do the hunting, not the people.

This will depend on the type of terrain

What kind of horse is best for fox hunting?

and the type of obstacles to be negotiated. In open types of country, such as the broad moors in parts of England and in Virginia, there is little brush, the fields are big, the going fast

and most of the obstacles are long board fences where a number of people can jump at the same time. Here a fast-going Thoroughbred is suitable. But in New England, Canada and parts of Ireland the going is very rough. There is apt to be a lot of mud and members have to take their turn in jumping specially chosen or erected "panels." Here a horse that is part Thoroughbred and part draft is better. It is not as excitable and its legs will stand up longer under these conditions. The *hunter* is one of the most fortunate of horses. It has to go out only twice a week and then only during the winter months, and it dearly loves its job. The fox has a much better chance of survival than does the pheasant or the deer which are hunted on foot with guns. The fox is also far faster, stronger and craftier than the hounds which chase it across the fields and countryside.

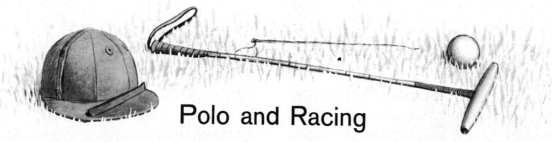

Polo and Racing

The game of polo probably originated

How did the game of polo develop?

in ancient Persia. The word itself means "ball." At first it was a sort of free-for-all with any number of players armed with crooked sticks trying to get the ball away from each other. When the English found themselves stationed in India they got some of the tough little *Mongolian* horses and trained them as polo

ponies. Gradually, regular rules were established.

In 1869, Lt. Hartopp, a member of the Tenth Hussars stationed in England, chanced to hear about the game. Fascinated, he and friends got out their army chargers and, armed with canes, tried hitting a small ball back and forth. Since this did not prove practical, the horses being too tall and the sticks too short, they then sent over to Ireland for some stout ponies. James Gordon Bennett is credited with introducing the game to the United States. He returned from England in 1876 with a supply of mallets, ponies were procured from Texas and games were started in Dickel's Riding Academy in New York City.

The rules of polo are much like those of field hockey. There **What is the object of the game?** are four players on each side and an umpire. The ball is thrown into the center. Then the members of

each team try, by hitting the ball from one to the other, to pass it down through the opposition's territory and between the goal posts. It is a rough game and since the ball is hard, the riders wear hard helmets and the horses, too, are protected with bandages on their legs.

A horse that is fifty-eight inches or less **What kind of horse is a polo pony?** is considered a pony, regardless of its breeding. Originally, no horse higher than thirteen hands and two inches (fifty-four

Polo, a kind of field hockey played on horseback, requires a high degree of skill from riders and horses both.

inches) was allowed to play in the game of polo. Today there is no such limitation, but naturally the smaller animals, provided they can carry the weight of the rider and are swift, are better. Arabian blood and *Quarter* horse blood as well as *Western Range* horse blood usually produce the desired type. The polo pony must be courageous, intelligent, sensitive (without being nervous or too high-strung), obedient, highly trained and must love the game. Polo ponies, after they have had a little schooling, soon learn to follow the ball for themselves.

The most famous story in literature about a polo pony is the one by Rudyard Kipling called *The Maltese Cat.*

A South American game, *pato,* meaning **What is the South American game of *pato?*** "duck," is called that because originally, though regrettably, a live duck was used instead of a ball. Pato is like mounted basketball. The round leather ball has a rope harness with handles. It is thrown through the air from one player to another. Here again small horses are preferable, for a good pato player expects to be able to sweep the ball up off the ground while traveling at a gallop.

The first race was probably between the **When and how did racing originate?** first two men who owned horses and liked to ride fast. Since those early days there have been many kinds of racing. The chariot races in Roman times were among the most exciting and most dangerous of sports. You have only to read the famous description in the book *Ben-Hur* by Lew Wallace and you will quickly understand how this is true.

But modern racing, as an organized sport, is far younger than either polo or fox hunting. It started with "demonstration" races held at the sales stables

The Roman chariot races were spectacles staged before huge audiences in open arenas.

Man O'War, one of the most famous race horses of all time, won $250,000 for its owner.

Still called "The Sport of Kings," horse racing has developed, over the years, into a thriving world-wide institution.

so that the auctioneers and sales owners could demonstrate the speed and stamina of their horses to prospective customers.

But King Henry VIII was really the father of racing. Not only did he keep a stable of race horses, but he required that the nobles and archbishops do the same and that they have frequent races for the entertainment of all.

What breed of horse is used in racing?

Were it not for this desire for excessive speed, the Thoroughbred horse would probably never have been developed as it has been. Early breeders discovered that if they crossed the fleet little Arabian with the larger European horse they got an animal that, because of its length of leg, had a longer stride

29

The horse supports itself alternately on the left and right legs in a pace. Its legs move in diagonal pairs in a trot. Both pacers and trotters are Standardbreds used in harness racing.

than the Arabian and so could cover more ground in a shorter time. Every horse that races today is directly descended from one of the three Arabian stallions imported for this purpose. No horse is allowed to run on a flat track without being a registered Thoroughbred.

Racing today is big business and the race horses are the celebrities of the horse kingdom. Enormous breeding establishments are located in nearly all countries. The owner of a mare that has had a good record on the track decides on a stallion of equally "royal" blood and high performance. The resulting offspring, the foal, will go to the trainers at the age of eighteen months, having

What is the life of a race horse like?

spent its babyhood in luxury. After a few months of training it will start its racing as a two-year-old. If it has a good record it will race only a few years. Then it will be retired to the stud farm. Stallions which have proved their worth bring tremendous prices. Tulyar, a famous Irish stallion, was sold to the Irish Government by the Aga Khan for $750,000 and later went to an American syndicate for even more. The famous Man O' War, hero of the American track, was probably the greatest race horse of our time.

But there are many types of racing other than flat racing. The *steeplechaser*, called *chaser* for short, races over obstacles on an oval track. The *point-to-point* horse is

What are the other types of racing?

30

really a hunter with speed. It races across country over natural obstacles such as banks, ditches, hedges, fences and stone walls. These races get their names from the custom of one man challenging a neighbor to race across country, going from one "point" to another, each rider being able to pick his own route. Since church steeples were prominent landmarks, the horses became known as "steeplechasers" or "point-to-pointers." The English Grand National is the most famous of the point-to-point type of race. It is run over a course with very high obstacles, and the horses that have won it most often over the years have been horses ridden by women.

How did trotting races start? The Puritans who colonized New England did not approve of racing and it was forbidden, although trotting was not prohib-

ited. Farmers and other horse-owners began the practice of challenging their neighbors to a trial of speed up and down the village streets—a sport which came to be known as "brushes." These were usually driving races, though some of the very early trotting races were under the saddle and for very long distances, even as far as from New York to Boston.

Society soon took up the new sport and in the late 1800's sections of old Harlem and parts of Long Island in New York were reserved on winter Sunday afternoons for those who, dressed in costly furs and driving high-stepping horses to their sleighs, tore up and down to the delight of spectators. A number of different breeds of horses came into being because of these races, and certainly racing, more than any other thing, is responsible for the development of the Thoroughbred as well as some of its lesser cousins.

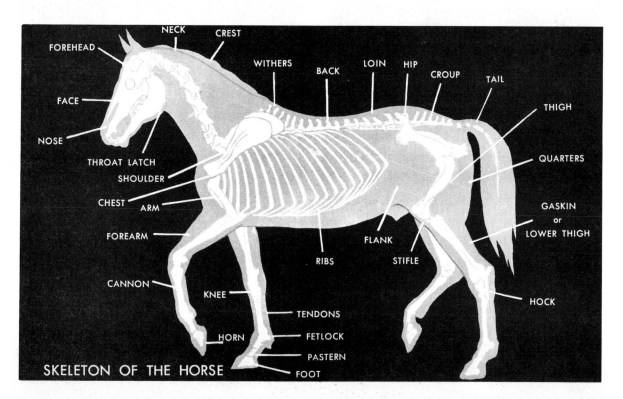

SKELETON OF THE HORSE

How the Horse Was Trained

When did man first train horses? No one knows the exact answer to this question. The earliest record we have was engraved on five stone tablets by Kikkulis, stable master for the king of the Hittites in the country of Mitanni in Asia Minor. These tablets were engraved in 1400 B.C. They are a day-to-day routine of how the horses of the king were to be selected, trained and conditioned. From the knowledge, obviously born of experience, that these tablets present, we realize that systematic training of the horse must have been studied many centuries before the time of Kikkulis.

For what purposes were horses trained? The horses of the Hittites pulled chariots both in racing and in war. They had to be swift, strong, bold, obedient and sturdy. Kikkulis, as well as the authorities of today, recommended that promising young horses from which the best would later be selected should be brought in from pasture and conditioned slowly. He told exactly what their daily ration of hay, grass, salt and grain should be and how it was to be increased slowly. He wrote that the first day, the horse must be walked exactly so many meters. Later, it is to be walked so many and trotted so many. Finally, the horse is to be galloped, but only when its muscles have been strengthened by exercise. Meanwhile, each day it is to be taken to the river, bathed seven times, allowed to roll in the sand and then thoroughly groomed and blanketed. When the band of horses under training have reached a certain stage and are in good condition, Kikkulis puts them all to the severe test of first being starved and deprived of water for forty-eight hours, then being worked under battle conditions at speed for twenty-four hours. Only those horses which could best withstand this severe test were chosen for the royal stables.

Who wrote the first book on training horses? Xenophon, the Greek writer, lived in 400 B.C. and his book is the first real work we have on training horses and riders. He was indeed a master and well understood the strengths and weaknesses of the horse. He realized that basically the horse is timid. Yet, if the horse was to be of use in warfare, it must be made bold. Xenophon knew that the animal must be brought to a high degree of training in obedience and agility. He knew that if the rider were to get the most out of his mount, the

GREEK
DRINKING HORN

The white Lippizans of Austria are the ballet dancers of the horse family and are noted as performing show horses.

To perform the movements called *dressage*, teamwork is required of a horse and rider.

PASSAGE

CAPRIOLE

COURBETTE

LEVADE

Horses performing in a circus obey each signal given by their trainer.

horse must be a willing partner, not just a fearful slave. "One cannot expect that a dancer will leap his highest in the best fashion and with grace if he is whipped with sharp brambles," writes Xenophon. So he recommended that the courage of the young horse be developed by such methods as leading it through the public streets on market days until it became accustomed to the strange sights and sounds and no longer feared them.

As a result of Xenophon's influence the Greeks trained their horses with firmness but gentleness. Their horses reached a high degree of perfection as did the riders in the art of horsemanship.

The Romans were not as wise as the Greeks when it came to horses. They did not put in the long hours necessary in training a horse to obey willingly, but used harsh bits, sharp rowels and the slashing of the whip to get their results. They were not interested in seeing the horse perform difficult and high leaps gracefully until, as Xenophon had said, the performance of man and horse might be compared to the art and grace of the dance. They were interested solely in chariot racing where only strength and courage were necessary. Under the Romans, the art of horsemanship and the development of the training of the horse deteriorated.

Did the Romans train horses?

An American cowboy works with his mount. The horse is trained to respond to slight indications of changing gait or to directions given by the rider's weight.

How did the masters of the Middle Ages train horses?

The art of horsemanship and the training of horses was a very important part of the life of every man during the Middle Ages. Most knights trained their own horses. Kings, lords and noblemen had professional horsemen who took over the training. We have a number of books on the subject by these various masters. The earlier ones followed the methods of the Romans and recommended cruel methods and harsh bits. Some of the bits used in the mouths of the horses of those days had sharp roweled wheels in them. Holding a horse's head under water by force if it showed fear of crossing rivers was another brutal method used. But Antoine de Pluvinel, the Master of Horse to King Louis XIII, broke away from this system.

De Pluvinel's book, *L'Instruction du*

Roi (The Instruction of a King), is fully illustrated with beautiful copperplate engravings and is written in the form of a dialogue between the author as master and the king as pupil. The author carried the training of the horse as far as it has ever been carried and his methods are still used in the famous Spanish Riding School of Vienna where Lippizan horses are trained.

Many men laughed at de Pluvinel for his methods and continued the old, brutal ways. Only in Spain, where the influence of the Arabs was still to be felt, was there a systematic method of training horses that was based on gentleness. Here, in 1605, a book by Luis de Bañuelos was published dealing with the Andalusian horse, its training and the training of the rider. De Bañuelos regretted that the youth of his day was becoming soft, that they were no longer good horsemen, but preferred instead

to ride about in carriages and to sell their highly trained animals to buy jewels for their lady friends. He quoted his grandfather who, at the age of ninety-four, always kept his horse saddled and waiting at the gate for him.

In 1733, another Frenchman named de la Guérinère published a cavalry manual called *The Understanding, Instruction and Care of the Horse.* He followed closely the maxims and methods of Xenophon and de Pluvinel. His goal was the making of a calm, obedient, agile and powerful mount that would always be under the complete control of its master and be his willing servant. His book had a very great influence on the training of the horse.

Before the year of 1900 in the United States, horses **What was the first book on horses in the United States?** were used for work purposes and for sport, but there was no interest in the higher development of horsemanship. The first writing we find on the subject published in the United States was a book called *Riding and Driving* by Edward I. Anderson and Price Collier in 1900. It shows that the authors had studied the advanced training of the horse seriously and applied the correct principles to the methods they advised.

Necessity was the cause of even very primitive peoples to learn to **What training was given the horse in the American West?** train their horses for specific purposes. The American Indians and the ancient Assyrians could ride

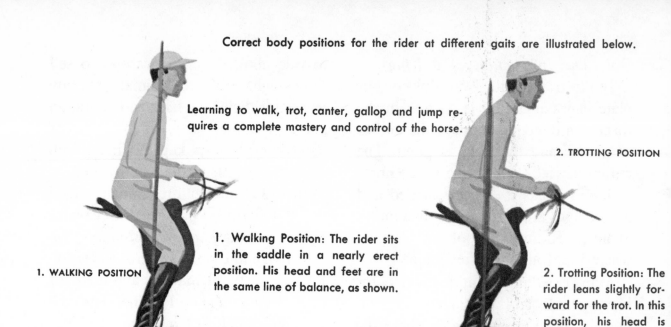

Learning to walk, trot, canter, gallop and jump requires a complete mastery and control of the horse.

1. WALKING POSITION

2. TROTTING POSITION

1. Walking Position: The rider sits in the saddle in a nearly erect position. His head and feet are in the same line of balance, as shown.

2. Trotting Position: The rider leans slightly forward for the trot. In this position, his head is out of the balance line.

There are several acceptable ways of mounting and dismounting. One is pictured.

MOUNTING
or
DISMOUNTING

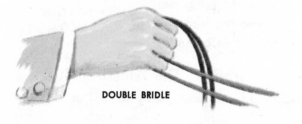

SNAFFLE BRIDLE

(Above): The way to hold the rein of a snaffle bridle. (Below): The curb rein is held between the little and ring fingers when using a double bridle.

DOUBLE BRIDLE

extremely well, controlling their horses in battle without reins and with only signals of the weight and legs. The American cowboy as well as range riders in other countries who used horses in their work also developed successful methods. The horse was taught to help the man herd cattle, driving them from one pasture land to another, and to separate desired animals that could be lassoed for branding and medical treatment. Like the Indian ponies, the animals were taught to respond instantly to slight indications of changing gait or to directions given by the rider's weight. Like the polo pony, they soon learned the game and would cut out the desired animal from a herd of milling beasts with little help from the rider who was busy manipulating his lariat.

But highly trained as these animals became, they cannot be compared in training to the horses of modern times which respond with incredible skill and strength to the direction of expert horsemen. It should be pointed out, however, that there is a vast difference in the

3. Canter Position: The canter, a kind of easy gallop, requires greater weight ahead of the balance line than in the walk and trot. The rider hollows his back and stays in balance with the horse's forward motion.

4. Gallop Position: The gallop, one of the horse's natural gaits, is a leaping motion. The rider flattens his body so that it is in a far forward position. More weight is put on the stirrups than in cantering.

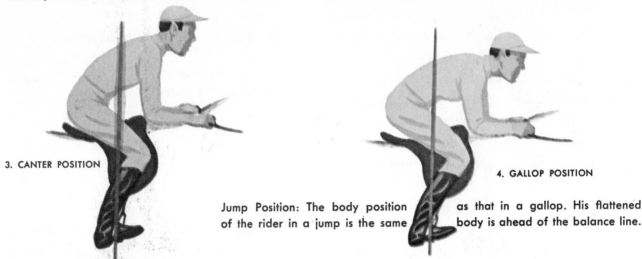

3. CANTER POSITION

4. GALLOP POSITION

Jump Position: The body position of the rider in a jump is the same as that in a gallop. His flattened body is ahead of the balance line.

horse trained for *dressage* and the circus-trained horse. Dressage is the guiding of a horse through maneuvers without emphasis on the use of reins, hands and feet. The mount is taught only to perform movements which all animals perform naturally. The circus-trained horse, however, is taught artificial movements.

Early in the twentieth century, an

What changes have taken place in racing, hunting and jumping?

Italian, Federico Caprilli, made a great contribution to the art of horsemanship in relation to jumping and fast work across country. Like most of the experts he was interested in improving the horses of the cavalry. He wanted to figure out how fast a horse could go over rough ground and how high it could jump while carrying a man. He studied the movements of the horse in the field and decided that when traveling at high speed and when jumping obstacles, the weight of the horse should

At one time, nearly everyone rode with his legs this way (above). But today, this is considered the best position of the legs in the stirrups (pictured below).

be on its forehand instead of on its center or on its hindquarters. He also decided that instead of sitting deep in the saddle at the gallop and over jumps, the rider, in order to relieve the horse of as much weight as possible, should stand in his stirrups and keep his own center of gravity over that of the horse instead of on its back. The Spanish writer de Bañuelos also mentions this.

At about the same time an American jockey named Tod Sloan had discovered the same thing and was winning races all over the country as well as abroad by shortening his stirrups and leaning far forward over the horse's neck. People laughed at him and said he rode like a "monkey on a stick," but before long all the other jockeys were copying him.

In 1936, another Italian named Piero Santini brought out a book called *The Forward Impulse* extolling Caprilli's method. Almost immediately this forward position for jumping was adopted by cavalry schools all over the world, as well as in the Olympic Games. Indeed,

many had adopted this method years before, but Santini's work popularized it.

Which American contributed much to horsemanship? There have been many American writers dealing with horsemanship since the time of Anderson and Collier. Some books have been good and some simply have been restatements of what other masters have said in print. The best known work is that by General Harry D. Chamberlin who, with some other army officers, was sent all over Europe to study methods of riding and training. He wrote several books, the most detailed being the cavalry manual *Horsemanship and Horsemastership*. He recommended a modified form of the Italian forward seat in which the rider balances over his stirrups without coming quite so far out of the saddle. He utilized the methods developed by the great masters, and recommended that the field horse and officers' chargers have a certain amount of dressage training as well as cross-country work and jumping.

In reviewing the history of the training of the horse, beginning with Kikkulis in 1400 B.C., one notices two things. Had it not been for the use of the horse in warfare, the animal would probably never have reached a very high degree of training. And though civilizations have changed, the horse has remained the same, and the same methods extolled by Xenophon are those that are still the most practical today.

Arabian colt. Arabians probably originated in India.

Modern Horses and Breeding

The Arabs have been keeping records

How did the Arabs improve the quality of their horses?

of the blood lines of their horses for about two thousand years. All Arabian horses spring from the blood of one of five mares, but there are very few Arabian horses that have been kept true to one of these strains. The Arabs discovered that if they chose a stallion and a mare with no serious defects, the colt would have the good qualities of both parents and be better than either. But if the mare and stallion had defects, then these would be worse still in the offspring. They also discovered that if horses to be mated were related to each other by blood — called "inbreeding" — then the best tendencies of the parents would be multiplied in the offspring.

By inbreeding — but always being very careful that the ancestors of the animals to be mated had the best possible characteristics — the Arabian horse of today has been produced. It is characterized by extreme intelligence, a high spirit but great docility, sensitivity, unusual strength in its wind and in the hardness of its feet, and the thickness and solidity of its bone structure. The animal is very swift and moves quickly, though its stride is shorter than the Thoroughbred's.

MORGAN

PALOMINO

Breeders of many different types of

How does Arab blood in other strains of horses affect them?

horses purposely introduce Arabian blood into their herds by keeping a purebred Arabian stallion. The general effect is to bring out in the foal the best qualities possessed by the mare as well as to increase its intelligence and sensitivity. Strangely enough, though the Arabian is a small horse, the introduction of its blood makes the offspring larger. And as we learned earlier, the crossing of the European mares with the Arabian stallions produced the Thoroughbred.

The word *thoroughbred* spelled with a

What is a Thoroughbred?

small "t" means purebred. A *purebred* is a breed of horse that has been kept pure for several generations. The word *Thoroughbred* spelled with a capital "T" is a

40

ARABIAN

TENNESSEE WALKING HORSE

AMERICAN SADDLE HORSE

special breed of horse, completely different from any other breed. All Thoroughbreds (the breed) trace their ancestry back to three original sires which were imported into England from Arabia between the years 1690 and 1725. Their names were the *Darley Arabian,* the *Byerly Arabian* and the *Godolphin Barb.* (A Barb is one species of Arabian.) Practically all of the other breeds also trace their ancestry back to these same stallions. The *Western Mustang* and modern range horse do not, but they do go back to other Arabian blood.

There are several other breeds of horses found in the United States. The **What other breeds are found in the U. S.?** most important are the *Standardbreds* (the horses that race in harness at the trot or pace), the *American Saddle horses,* the *Morgans,* the *Quarter*

41

horses, the *Tennessee Walkers* and the *Western Range horse* or cow pony.

The Puritans, who believed it sinful to race, defined a race as a contest between horses which were being made to run as fast as possible. As trotting was not a racing gait, horses that entered into contests at this gait could not be said to be racing. Farmers and others soon found it was fun to race their neighbors, both under the saddle and in harness at the trot, and they used either Thoroughbreds or crossbred horses that happened to trot well.

Then, in 1849, a crippled mare destined **Which stallion was born of a crippled mare?** for the slaughterhouse was bought, out of pity, by a farmer. Known later as the Kent Mare, she was bred to a stallion named Abdallah whose lineage traced back to the Darley Arabian through a very famous stallion named Messenger. The colt that was the result of this mating, and its mother, were sold by the farmer to his farm hand, Bill Rysdyk, for a "promise-to-pay" note, and later, this same colt was to become world-famous as Hambletonian.

Hambletonian raced only a few times before the horse was retired for stud purposes. It was discovered that the offspring of the celebrated mount, without exception, all had powerful trots, and today, the name Hambletonian has come to be almost synonymous with Standardbred or trotter. Practically all the horses on the trotting tracks today go back to this famous sire.

Hambletonian (after an old Currier and Ives print).

In trotting, the horse moves its diagonal
legs together in
pairs. For exam-
ple, the right hind
leg and the left
foreleg work together. The footprint of
the back foot is well in advance of that
of the front foot. This means that the
horse must have tremendously strong
hind quarters with long ligaments. Also,
most racing trotters spread their back
legs to bypass the front feet and so
avoid cutting themselves. This gives a
sort of rotating movement to the gait.
The trot of a Standardbred does not
look at all like the trot of any other type
of horse and is not only extraordinarily
fast, but also very smooth.

**What are the
leg movements of
a racing trotter?**

The *pacers* were developed from the
trotting stock. The pace
is a gait in which the two
legs on the same side
move together instead of the diagonal
legs. Pacers go very fast and most are
rough to ride. Some develop the gait
naturally, while some are trained to
pace by means of hobbles, which prevent them from trotting. The pacers
also go back to Hambletonian.

**What are
pacers?**

The plantation owners who lived in Virginia, Ken-
tucky and
other south-
ern states
managed plantations of several thousand acres. This meant that they often
spent long days in the saddle riding
from one part of the property to another, inspecting the crops, talking to
the overseers and so forth. But they

**How did the
American Saddle horse
come into being?**

Trot: Horse moves diagonal legs together in pairs.

Pace: The two legs on the same side move together.

were not only farmers. They were also
aristocrats who admired beautiful, sensitive, proud-looking, spirited horses.
But the Thoroughbred was too nervous,
too apt to step on young plants, and was
unwilling to stand patiently while its
master chatted. Furthermore, the trot,
the natural gait of the Thoroughbred,
was too tiring and the gallop was too
fast.

The Arabian horses were often taught
a gait known as a *rack* or *singlefoot*.
Unlike the trot and the pace, at this
gait the horse puts each foot down indi-
vidually, but in quick succession. The
result is a movement of extreme smooth-
ness. Perhaps the Southern planters

43

Parade horses ridden in rodeos and other horse shows have been trained to execute various artificial gaits, in addition to the natural movements of the horse.

Some principal gaits of a horse are seen below.

CANTER

TROT

WALK

would have chosen Arabians to ride, but they were difficult to get at the time, since the Arabs did not like to sell them, and when they did, transportation problems in those days increased the difficulty. But in 1850, a Thoroughbred named Denmark was put at stud in Kentucky. It had some of the same ancestry as Hambletonian, but whereas Hambletonian's colts all turned out to be trotters or pacers, Denmark's offspring all took to the rack, or single-foot. This famous horse became the great foundation sire of the breed known as the *American Saddle horse*.

The *Saddler* is a beautiful animal with

How does the Saddler differ from other breeds?

a fine, delicate head, proudly held on a long, arched neck. Its body, or barrel, is short, its quarters are powerful and its tail is set very high. The saddler picks up its feet so high that sometimes, at the rack and trot, its knees almost hit the chest. Its canter is very slow and short and smooth.

There are two types of Saddle horse. One, the *five-gaited* variety, wears a long flowing mane and a long flowing tail. In horse shows, you sometimes see five-gaited horses with false tails if the natural tail is scanty. It must show a flat-footed walk, a "slow gait" which may be a running walk, a fox trot or broken amble, a trot, a rack and a canter. The rack is the fastest and in

STEPPING PACE

RACK

the horse shows, when the crowds shout "Rack on, Rack on," the horse's feet move so fast that they hardly seem to touch the ground at all. Five-gaited horses are sometimes shown first under saddle and then in harness. They are then known as *combination* horses.

The *three-gaited* Saddle horse is a lighter-built animal. It wears its mane cut off entirely and its tail pulled until there's hardly any hair left at all. It is only required to show the walk, trot and canter.

Who was Justin Morgan? Justin Morgan was a school teacher who was born in West Springfield, Massachusetts in 1747. His name is known and will probably be remembered for many generations among horse lovers because he was the owner of a stocky, plucky little

stallion which bore his name. *Justin Morgan* the horse was the only stallion to become the sire of a distinctive breed of horse whose members are all known today by this name. The exact ancestry of this unusual animal is not entirely clear and probably never will be.

There is a monument to Justin Morgan which was given to the United States Department of Agriculture by the Morgan Horse Club. It is a large statue of the famous stallion, and it stands in the famous Morgan Stud Farm in Middlebury, Vermont. The farm is maintained by the Department of Agriculture for the purpose of improving farm horses and to breed Morgans. The statue shows a short-legged, long-barreled, muscular little animal, which would be called a "pony" today, since it is only fourteen hands and two inches. It has an Arabian type head, held very high, an enormous chest and bunchy, powerful muscles.

Police use Morgans to patrol city streets, parks and shoreline areas.

The *Quarter horse* gets its name from the fact that it is a race horse that runs only a quarter of a mile. In colonial days, the planters of Virginia dearly loved racing, and there was no prohibition against it as there was in New England. But neither were there any big oval tracks where horses could go around and around for several miles. However, in various parts of the state there were winding trails, wide enough for several horses to travel abreast. These were short—about a quarter of a mile. So the Virginia gentlemen began selecting as breeding stock, animals which could get off to a rapid start and turn readily.

Where did the Quarter horse get its name?

Most of the offspring of a Thoroughbred called Janus seemed to have these qualifications, so Janus became the founder, or Foundation Sire, of the breed. Then the coming of the race track took away the need for a horse that ran only a quarter of a mile, and Quarter horses were no longer bred for racing. But powerful, fast-turning animals were just what the cowboy needed in his work with cattle and they were also valuable to those breeding polo ponies. It is for these reasons that Quarter horses are bred today.

The Quarter horse has very bunchy muscles, especially in its hind quarters, upper legs and jaws. It does not carry its head very high, but seems to have most of its weight in the forehand. It is powerful and heavy, and weighs much more

What does a Quarter horse look like?

than horses far taller than itself. However, the horse is by no means clumsy.

The modern stock horse, or cow pony, used as a working animal on the ranches in the West and South and in rodeos, is a type rather than a breed. The original western horse, the mustang, was descended from the Spanish horses brought over by Cortez and others. But these horses deteriorated somewhat in size because of the scanty food and rough, mountainous country. In the past hundred years, the ranch-owners have been introducing Morgan, Quarter horse, Arabian and Thoroughbred blood into their herds by having purebred stud horses of those breeds. In so doing, they have improved the range horse in size and strength as well as in agility.

Is the cow pony a distinct breed?

The *Tennessee Walker*, sometimes called the *Plantation Walker*, is of mixed Saddle and Morgan ancestry or Quarter horse. It was bred to give the plantation owners a quiet ride, to walk, canter and to go at

What is a Tennessee Walker?

Endurance, skill and speed are notable in cow ponies.

a "slow-gait" in such a manner that it would not endanger the crops when ridden between the rows. It was also used for light farm work. Today there are classes for Tennessee Walkers in many of the big shows and the breed is very popular as a "pleasure horse" for people who just ride for fun.

The palomino is a color, and not a breed. There is a registry for palominos, but horses of many different types of ancestry are eligible provided they are of the desired golden color with a white mane and tail. Thus far, no one has been able to be certain of reproducing the required color by breeding two palominos.

Is the palomino a breed?

The donkey is a member of the *Equus,* or horse family, but the animal evolved differently and is not a true horse. It has been bred and used for many centuries as a pack, farm and riding animal. The donkey is easy to keep, being able to fend for itself where there appears to be practically nothing edible to be found, it can work long hours, and

What are donkeys?

The American Saddle horse displays elegant bearing.

it is seldom sick or lame. The animal is an incredibly strong little beast, hardly larger than St. Bernard dogs, and it can bear loads that weigh over two hundred fifty pounds. Donkeys are valued as pets and are often the first mounts for children. They are also known as *asses* and *burros.*

The mule is the result of mating a male donkey with a female horse. It is large, strong, somewhat stubborn, sluggish and easy to keep. The mule gets its size from the female parent, but everything else from the male. A *jennet,* an animal not very common today, but well known in medieval times, is the result of mating a small pony stallion with a donkey mare. The jennet takes after the horse side of the family, having a finer coat, silkier tail and a more slender build than that of donkeys. From the female parent, the jennet inherits a smooth gait and a patient disposition. Ladies of the Middle Ages usually preferred to ride them, rather than horses. Since it is rare for mules or jennets to have offspring, there is no way of reproducing them except through cross-breeding.

What are mules?

The zebra is descended from the prehistoric horse. Its unusual "protective" coloring — the stripes—was a chance happening during the animal's development in Africa, and is useful in aiding the zebra to conceal itself in grass. It is hard to tame, but those raised in captivity are easily trained to drive. Zebras have one characteristic which is

What are zebras?

47

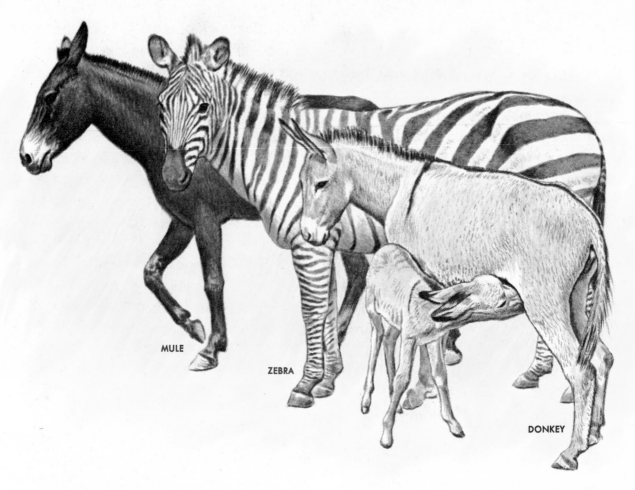

MULE

ZEBRA

DONKEY

different from horses. Like the horse, it is a herd animal, roaming in small herds with a stallion in charge. But unlike the horse, the zebra is often found together with other animals—the ostrich or gnu, for example. But these animals would only be grazing in the same area.

Though the horse is no longer essential in farming, transportation or warfare, it will **What is the future of the horse?** be centuries before the animal disappears entirely. Its two main activities today are sport and pleasure. Fox hunting will probably die out before any of the other sports for which horses are used, because of the increased building which has limited field space. But today, many horses are still used for this purpose.

Polo and racing continue to attract crowds, and the sport of racing requires the breeding of more horses than ever before. Horse show competitions have multiplied greatly in the past twenty-five years. And international competitions, including the Olympic Games, are gaining in popular interest.

The children of today are even more fascinated by the horse than those of two generations ago. More and more children and young people are studying riding seriously with the idea of entering competitions or becoming breeders, instructors or even horse veterinarians.

The value of the horse to the human race was well expressed by a book character who said, "There is something about the outside of the horse that is good for the inside of the man."